How to Use a Sewing Machine for Beginners

Step By Step Guide On How to Start Using a Sewing Machine as a Complete Beginner

Introduction

Perhaps you would really love to sew but don't really know how to start, or maybe you have found a sewing machine in your grandma's attic, and you want to get that thing revved up so that you can make yourself some nice lanyard or something. Whatever your reasons are for wanting to sew, you've come to the right place.

This book contains everything (literally) you would need to know as someone new to sewing, including things such as your most suitable sewing machine, needles, threads and attachments to use, how to sew, caring for your machine, and so many more!

This book is suitable for you:

- *If you have never touched a sewing machine before but now want to know how to use one—or are curious about how to sew.*

- *You touched one and but really didn't understand how to use it, so you quit.*

- *You've used one, but you now want a deeper understanding of how to use a sewing machine like a pro sewist.*

- *You want to learn new or different seams, ruffles, hens, stitches, etc.*

With the right guide, sewing is easy, and trust me when I say that when you get into it and experience how much fun it is, you will love every bit of it!

Let's get started!

Table of Content

Section 1

The Ins and Outs Of
Your Sewing Machine

If you don't already have a sewing machine, you might be wondering which kind of machine you should get. There are many types of sewing machines available, from mechanical ones to computerized embroidery machines.

Although some sewing machines may differ in some way, fundamentally, all sewing machines serve the same purpose: *making a lockstitch using a bobbin thread and an upper thread to fuse two layers of fabric.*

The Anatomy Of Your Sewing Machine

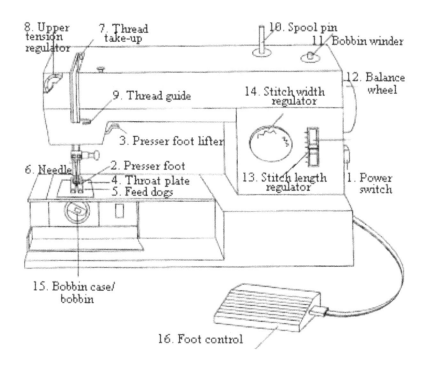

Your sewing machine will have the following parts:

1: Hand wheel/balance wheel/fly wheel

You will use this to operate the machine by hand and turns when you press the foot pedal. When winding bobbins, the hand wheel automatically disengages on computerized machines. With most mechanical sewing machines, you will have to do this manually.

2: Reverse control

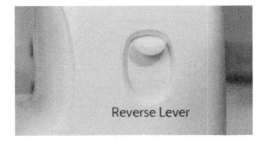

This part turns the feed dog in the opposite direction moving the fabric towards you as you sew- it locks in the stitches.

3: Spool pins

Spool pins can either be vertical or horizontal; they hold the thread on the sewing machine. Most machines have two of them to allow for the use of two threads at the same time.

4: Bobbin winder and Bobbin winder stop

Bobbin winder stop, as the name suggests, stops the bobbin from winding once it is full.

The actual bobbin winder holds the bobbin in place when you are wounding the thread onto it.

5: Stitch pattern library

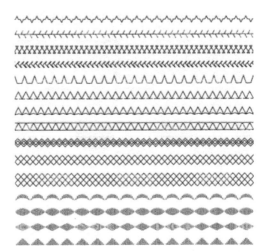

This diagram illustrates all the stitches that the machine can make. The number depends on that particular machine.

6: A foot pedal

When you press down on the foot pedal, you can operate the machine. Some machines are computerized such that they have a power button to operate the machine automatically.

7: *Stitch length and width*

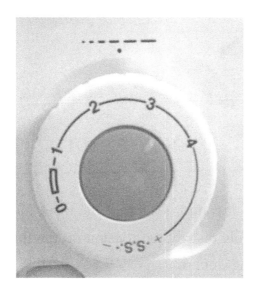

The stitch length control sets the speed of the feed dog compared to the needle. The longer your stitch is, the faster the feed dog pulls through the fabric, and the farther apart the stitches become. For most modern machines, they measure from 0 to ⅟16" (0 to 4 mm), while some high-end machines can go up to ¼" (6 mm).

The stitch width regulates how far the needle can move from the center to the right or the left. Adjusting the width of the stitch can also change the position of the needle to the right or left to stitch straight if the machine doesn't have a different needle position adjuster.

8: Bobbin winder tension

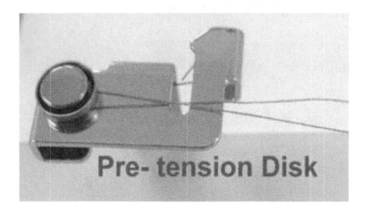

These are small round disks that the thread passes between to ensure evenly distributed tension on the thread when the bobbin is being wound.

9: Upper and lower thread guides

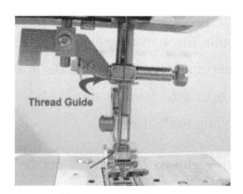

When the thread leaves the spool pin, it passes through the upper thread guide and also before it passes through the tension disks.

All sewing machines have a lower thread guide right above the needle for helping the thread go down the fabric with the needle. Some machines have extra bonus guides above the needle guide.

10: Pattern selector dial

You turn this dial to select the symbol of your required stitch pattern. For computerized machines, you can select the pattern on a menu screen.

11: Thread take-up lever

The thread passes through here after going through the tension disks. The thread take-up lever moves up and down with the needle, and it should be in the highest position at the start and end of a seam to avoid thread tangling.

12: Tension dial and disks

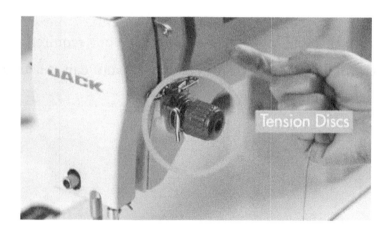

These two are usually found together, and your thread goes between these two metal disks. The tension disk controls the speed of the thread from the top, and the dial ranges tension from 0 to 9 (0 is the loosest and 9 is the tightest).

NOTE: The tension is usually set to 4 as tighter tension slows the thread down as the disks come closer together, and looser tension spreads the disks far apart such that more room is created for the thread to pass through faster.

13: Needle plate/throat plate/face plate and feed dog

A needle plate has a hole for the needle to pass through, and it also has markings to guide you with the seams. A feed dog pulls fabric through the machine.

14: Presser foot

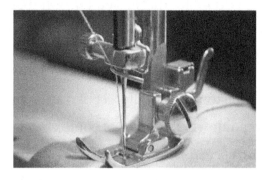

This part simply holds the fabric against the feed dog.

15: Extension table and box

These attachments are removable for free-arm sewing when you are sewing narrow tubes such as sleeves and hems of trousers. You can also remove them to allow access to front-load bobbins.

16: A needle

The needle goes into the fabric to connect the threads.

Types Of Sewing Machines

There are many types of sewing machines out there, but the general rule of thumb is, the more the functions and stitches, the more expensive it will be.

Some types of sewing machines include:

Manual sewing machines

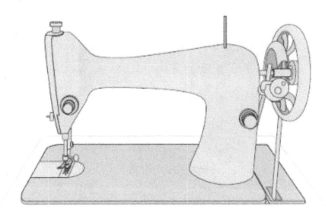

These are operated using a hand wheel operated with one hand or using your foot to pump on a treadle. These machines can only perform basic stitching, and for such straightforward stitching, they are adequately perfect (but can be a bit slow).

These machines are sturdy, simple to service, and don't have problems; they are also ideal if there isn't a reliable electric supply.

Manual sewing machine factors to consider

- If you are getting a second-hand machine, ensure it is still in great condition, and that replacement needles are available.

- If you are extremely environmentally conscious, this is the ideal sewing machine to get.

- Some super old machines can only stitch chain stitch instead of lockstitch (not a very secure stitch).

- A handheld battery-driven machine may be fine for a simple repair job or a straight seam, but you won't be able to do some serious sewing with it.

Electric sewing machines

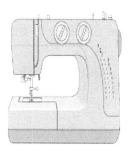 

This machine has a motor in its body that moves the needle as it coordinates it with the motion of the feed dog and bobbin below the needle plate. With this motor, usually steered by a foot pedal, the harder you press your foot, the faster you sew (foot pedal allows you to have your hands free for guiding the fabric).

You select the type of stitch, length, and width through the turning dials.

Electrica sewing machine factors to consider

- When you settle on an electric machine, know that it won't be possible to add more functions or stitches later, so ensure that the machine you settle on can do everything you want to do.

- Electric machines are more accurate and faster than manual models.

- Some old electric machines had their stitch patterns on a small pattern disc. If you find such, make sure it has a good selection as it will be difficult to find more.

- Even for electric machines, check its condition if it is a second-hand machine.

-

Computerized sewing machines

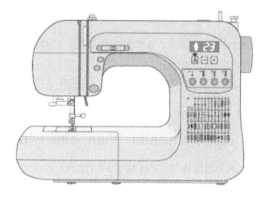

These sewing machines have more stitches to offer than electric machines and usually allow for additional functions that let you create your unique simple patterns.

These machines have several motors that power different functions that offer precise control, making it possible to create hundreds of different stitches. The machines also have computer chips with the right tension, width, and length for each stitch installed by the manufacturer—they're also adjustable to create certain effects.

All you need to do is select your desired stitch by pressing a key or using a touchpad. To add to this, you can store stitches or copy extra stitches from a memory card or CD or download them yourself!

Computerized sewing machine factors to consider

- If you need to connect your machine to a computer, make sure you have a compatible model.

- Be realistic about the number of functions and stitches you will need; it's better to spend your money on a better quality machine than one with hundreds of functions/stitches you won't need.

- Check the clarity of the LCD screen. Can you easily read what's on the screen?

- If you will need to add further stitches later, ensure your machine allows for this.

Embroidery machine

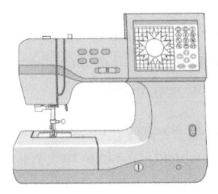

Usually designed for embroidery, but embroidery sewing machine models have general sewing functions too. Basic embroidery machines generally stitch all parts of your embroidery design in a single color and then stop until the next color is threaded on.

Some other expensive machines can automatically switch between different color threads added at the beginning. These machines (all embroidery machines) also offer motifs and borders, and you can usually purchase new designs and add as required. You can also create your unique designs using design software on your computer.

Embroidery sewing machine factors to consider

- A combination sewing/embroidery machine is more compact than having two different machines. Therefore, if you don't want to take up a lot of space, get a machine that can do both.

- If you want to stitch large motifs, check the maximum embroidery area the machine can handle.

- Check maximum embroidery area if you would want to be stitching large motifs.

- Again if you will be using computer design software, ensure that it's compatible with your model.

- If the machine utilizes several colors simultaneously, an automatic threading feature will save you a lot of time.

A serger

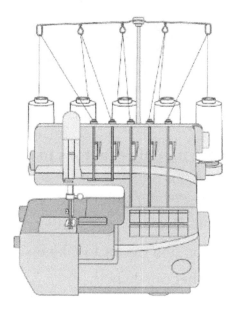

Also called an overlock machine, a serger can stitch, trim, and finish the edge all at once, thereby giving your projects a professional finish.

This machine is way faster than a regular sewing machine for such tasks. However, it doesn't offer a well-rounded set of sewing functions, e.g., topstitching and buttonholes.

Nevertheless, if you will be sewing regularly, the serger is worth investing in for the seams and hems. Just opt to choose one that offers built-in functions and the likelihood of purchasing attachments.

Serger sewing machine factors to consider

- Some less expensive sergers have the problem of stretching fabric and having it pucker while you stitch; be keen on the model.

- A serger can't replace a regular sewing machine, but it will save you time spent on finishing raw edges; it also offers special effects creation, which makes it great if you will be sewing a lot.

- Go for a machine that has a differential feed to get additional sewing options. This differential will allow you to, for instance, speed up the feed to sew a ruffle on some woven fabric or form a waved edge effect.

- Some sergers utilize regular sewing machine needles while many need special needles; ensure you can get them easily.

- Don't give in to the temptation to get a lightweight, inexpensive serger. Sergers are, by design, meant to operate at quite a rate, so it needs to have some weight so that it can stay steady as you work. A light machine can jump around, which is dangerous and can ruin your work.

Features of a Great Sewing Machine

What makes a great sewing machine?

A high-quality sewing machine is a great asset that can last forever as long as you take care of it—we will discuss how later on.

Ideally, a good machine should possess the following features:

- The machine should be made mostly out of metal parts and strong plastic because weak plastic can break and crack over time.

- The machine should be quiet even when operating at high speeds.

- Your machine should have a multi-part feed-dog unit to offer a good grip on fabric and evenly pull it through.

- When choosing a machine, ensure that the hand wheel is turning smoothly without jamming or slipping.

- The foot pedal should be responsive and sensitive; ensure it doesn't slide around.

- Your presser foot's pressure should work as well on the thinnest silks as it does on denim and thick wools.

- The machine should have a good hook to always stop the threads from jamming in the bobbin at the start of a seam.

- Check the threading path and ensure that it is well-designed to prevent the threads from getting tangled or unthreaded.

- The machine should be significantly heavy to prevent it from moving around the table as you work with it, even at high speeds. The weight of a sewing machine is usually relative to its size and that of its motor, but ideally, the machine should weigh between 10-30 pounds (4.5-14 kg)

- Ensure that the timing between the bobbin threads and the needle thread is perfect to avoid skipped stitches. If you've found a machine you really like (or you already have one) and the timing seems off, you can always adjust it. You can do that by either aligning the top timing mark precisely below the base of the timing bar bushing or using the hand wheel to lower the needle completely and raising it 2.4mm (the needle eye should be 2.4mm below the location of the hook.

Section2

Your Sewing Spot

As you join the sewing world, you might take up projects that consume a lot of time to complete—now that you are learning how to sew, don't be surprised if all of your family members ask for quilts.

If we lived in a perfect world, all sewists would have some space where you can let everything spread out and continue from where you left off every time. If this isn't possible, you need to make room for your sewing spot.

Sewing Spot suggestions:

- Chose a spot that has as much natural light as possible.

- Your sewing space should have convenient electrical outlets for your machine, ironing, and task lighting.

- Find an unused corner you can use to store your equipment and work without disrupting your household.

- For your cutting table, use a folding decorator's table or two trestles to balance the board. Disassemble and store out of sight when not in use.

- If you are working in the dining room or a spare bedroom, build in sufficient storage so that you can keep your sewing projects and equipment away neatly when you need the room for other use.

- The eaves or the unused space under the stairs can be a great sewing spot—screens or folding doors can hide away your sewing clutter nicely.

Storage and Organization Tips

- If making a quilt, keep the quilt blocks flat in a box or shelf until you are ready to sew them up together.

- Hang up drapes and garments you are working on between your sewing sessions to ensure they don't crease.

- For small pieces of miscellaneous equipment, keep them in transparent containers so that you can see what you have easily—one with different compartments is best.

- Store wound bobbin and matching spool together by using a string to thread together both through the central hole and then knot the ends together.

- Keep small pieces of fabric in plastic, see-through crates, and have them lidded—this will allow you to see things easily without unpacking.

- For large lengths of fabric, store them in cardboard rolls and avoid folding because the weight of the layers is bound to form creases over time.

- Have your spools of thread in a storage box to make sure the ends don't tangle together. Keep large cones on racks made for that specific purpose.

Your Posture

If you will be working on your machine for long periods, ensure you have a chair that supports your back such that it is straight (at 90 degrees to your lower body). Your forearms should also be at 90 degrees to your body, and the bottom of your elbows should be the same level as the sewing bed. To attain this posture, you might need a lower table or a higher chair than normal.

You might also want to go for a chair with no arms and a straight back to avoid back/neck strain and support easier movement.

Have your foot control near your right foot and if your machine uses a kneebar, have this near your right knee.

Your Lighting

When it comes to sewing, the importance of good lighting can't (and shouldn't) be something you underestimate. Most sewing machines come with a built-in light that comes on once the machine switches on, but you also need an additional light source for your working area.

A flexible table lamp is your best option as you can position it as needed.

NOTE: When replacing built-in bulbs on your machine, ensure the replacements are the same type, wattage, and voltage as the old one—you want the same visibility.

Sewing Machine Storage

When not in use, make sure you cover your machine with a hard case or a soft cover to keep it dust-free and generally clean. You can then keep it away in a place of your convenience, such as the back of a wardrobe or under a table—make sure the place is dry.

Maintenance

Many modern sewing machines are, by design, as maintenance-free as possible, besides regular cleaning to ensure that dust and residue from thread and fabric don't build up (it can cause excess wear and tear).

When it comes to maintaining your sewing machine, generally:

- Make a habit of cleaning all the lint from your machine whenever you complete a project. Pay close attention to that area under the needle and around the bobbin mechanism and feed dog.

- Take out the needle plate/unlatch the access panel, remove the bobbin and the bobbin holder and use a small stiff lint brush (usually bundled with the machine) to clean fluff and lint from the bobbin holder and between the hook race and feed dog.

- Most modern machines don't need oiling; be sure to check the machine's manual first. If your sewing machine needs oiling, the manual will show where exactly. For older machines, the lubrication points may have some marking indicators on the machine.

When you oil your machine, use oil specifically made for a sewing machine. After oiling, sew some lines of stitches on junk fabric to let any excess oil flow out.

Servicing

It's best to leave servicing your machine to an approved technician according to warranty terms if it is still within its warranty period. After the period elapses, seek servicing from a service engineer and ensure you are dealing with a professional, especially if you have a computerized sewing machine.

Some servicing elements you should keep in mind include:

- **Heavy use:** If you use your machine five times a week, you need to do servicing once every year.

- **Moderate use:** If you use your machine moderately, say less than once a week, service it every two years.

- **Occasional use:** Even if you don't use your machine very often, ensure to have it checked out after every two years.

- **In case of an event:** Always send your machine for servicing if damaged or dropped, totally jammed up, or has become wet.

Section 3

Sewing Basics

Before we dive into the good stuff, here are a few things to check to make sure you have everything in order. Take time to go through the information below if you want to achieve that professional look with all your projects:

Marking and Measuring

Most sewing projects require accurate measuring. You can use many tools for measuring and marking, and although sometimes the fabric you are using and the kind of work you are doing can be factors, it all comes down to your preferences.

Measuring

The golden rule when measuring is: ***take every measurement twice!***

Measuring tools

The measuring tools you will need include:

- **Tape measure:** A tape measure suitable for sewing should be flexible and show both metric and imperial to save you from converting dimensions. The types you can use include:

  - Fiberglass tape: This is less likely to stretch with time.

- o Retractable metal tape measure: This is usually longer than a standard tape measure and is great when used to measure windows for drapes and projects alike.

- **Seam gauge:** A seam gauge is a small metal ruler that has a sliding marker. It will prove useful for measuring widths of the border and bringing out seams of even depth.

- **Yardstick:** The traditional use for this 1m wooden ruler (36 inches) is to measure fabric length. It also works great if you need to measure something above your head since it doesn't bend like a metal one.

- **Adjustable ruler:** This tool can fold out to a considerable length, and when you lock it in place, it becomes quite stable, making it handy for measuring high windows and under furniture where a tape measure can twist or buckle.

Marking

When you're marking, your want to make an inconspicuous yet visible mark that won't show on the finished project. You can try on either side of the fabric to determine which side is most suitable.

Marking tools

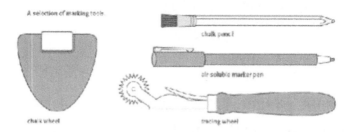

A selection of marking tools

chalk pencil

air soluble marker pen

chalk wheel

tracing wheel

- **A water-soluble marker:** Marks made with this marker can be easily sponged off with water or disappear on the first wash, making these markers suitable on only washable fabrics.

- **Air soluble marker:** Marks from an air soluble marker gradually fade from exposure to air, with the time it takes for the mark to fade varying according to the fabric. It might not be advisable for use on long projects as the marks can disappear too quickly.

- **Tailor's pencil/chalk pencil:** This is available in different colors, and it usually contains a stiff brush for removing marks when you don't need them anymore.

- **Chalk wheel:** This is an easy-to-use dispenser that you can refill with a variety of colors of chalk powder such that you can choose the appropriate color for your fabric.

- **Tracing wheel**: A dressmaker's carbon is what you place between the fabric and pattern, and the tracing wheel is run along the lines of the design to form a dotted outline on the fabric. It is an easy method for marking; however, the marks might be hard to remove; hence, it's best for designs you can hide with stitching.

Pinning

Pinning secures the pattern to the fabric as you cut, but it is also a great way to hold layers of fabric together as you stitch.

Pincushion and pins

For most fabrics, plain steel pins are ideal but when working with very delicate fabrics, find an extra-fine version of the pins. Find pins with a large colored head, which makes them easier to spot, and opt for glass pins over plastic ones to avoid melting in case you iron over them. You can also find extra-long pins if you need to hold layers of fabric together.

When it comes to holding your pins, a pincushion is ideal because of its ease of access when you need a pin in a hurry. You can also use a magnetic pin dispenser.

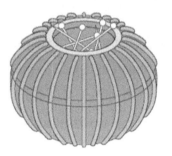

A magnetic pin dispenser.

Pinning a pattern

Before you start pinning, make sure you have your pattern pieces at hand.

1. A1 Cut out your required pieces and if the pattern paper is super creased, use a cool iron to press gently, then lay out the pieces on your fabric roughly.

2. A2 You will need to align most of the pieces with the straight grain of the fabric and mark it with a straight-of-grain line (this is normally a heavy line with arrowheads at both ends). Measure the distance between this line and the next selvage at each end, and pin the grain line in place.

3. A3 To ensure ultimate stability, place pins all around the edges of the pattern, ensuring you position the pins in a diagonal position in the corners. Before beginning to cut the patterns, pin all the pieces to the fabric first.

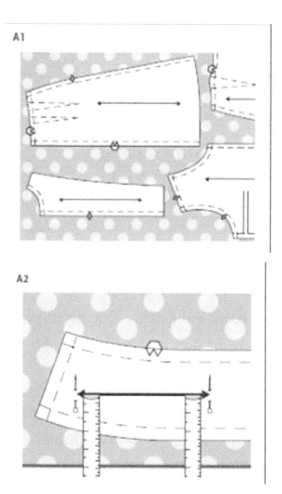

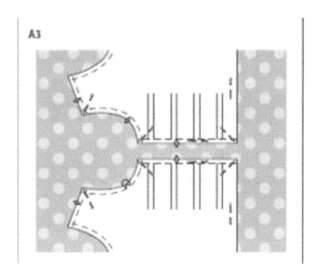

Pinning for machine sewing

Place your pieces of fabric together, keeping the raw edges aligned.

1. B1 Hold together the layers with pins at right angles to the edge. Position the heads in a way that makes it easy to remove the pins efficiently as you stitch: to the left, if left-handed, and to the right, if right-handed.

2. B2 if using a detachable seam guide, place the pins pointing towards the edge- the pin should never be next to the needle plate. On shaped edges or small projects, space your pins around 2.5cm to 7.5 cm apart (1 to 3 inches). On straight, long seams, have the pins a little further apart.

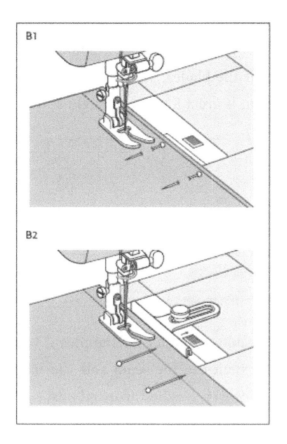

Pinning for serging

A serger has moving blades that will hook on the pin, dull the blades and even send metal fragments to either you or the machine (or both). Always take care not to stitch over a pin by keeping them far from your working area.

1. P1 Pin fabrics together with pins at right angles to the edge but ensure you remove them before coming close to the needle.

2. P2 Alternately, have your pins parallel to the stitching line but some distance away to make sure the pins are not near the blades. This method isn't ideal for detail areas but is great for long, straight seams.

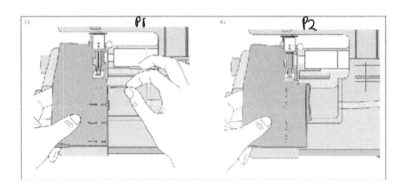

TIP: It is possible to stitch over the pins if you have placed them at right angles to the seam and you have the presser foot hinged; however, it is best to avoid this.

Cutting Sewing Fabric

The key to cutting fabric nicely and accurately is to ensure your scissors are sharp and the fabric is completely flat on the surface as you cut—it will make things much quicker and easier.

Before you measure your lengths, ensure you cut the raw end of the fabric on the straight-of-the-grain.

TIP: Always press the fabric flat and smooth to get rid of any folds or wrinkles.

Cutting tools

- **Dressmaker's shears or Fabric scissors:** Go for a pair that sits comfortably in your hand. Special dressmaker's shears usually have one handle at an angle to the blades to allow the blades to slide along whatever you are cutting in more of a horizontal position, thus keeping the fabric flat for more precise cutting.

- **Thread/embroidery scissors:** These scissors are small and have sharp points ideal for snipping threads, snipping into awkward corners, and fine detail fabric cutting.

- **Paper/regular scissors:** Always have a spare pair of regular scissors you can use to cut synthetic wadding and paper patterns and for other types of general cutting work.

- **Pinking shears:** These have notched blades, making them cut a zigzag line. They are great for trimming a raw seam to prevent fraying and to form a decorative edge.

- **Seam ripper:** This great tool has a sharp prong for pushing into stitches and a small sharp blade for slicing through the thread. You can use it to unpick seams quickly and cut slits for machine-stitched buttonholes.

Cutting fabric for a pattern

Paper patterns are delicate and can tear easily, which is why it is best to handle them carefully when pinning them to your fabric.

- Lay the pieces with the printed side up (unless instructed otherwise on the pattern cutting guide).

- If the cutting guide indicates the double thickness of fabric, tuck the fabric right sides together. And if the cutting guide indicates single thickness, have the fabric right side up and place the pattern on it with its printed side up; remember to turn the pattern piece over if you will cut the left and right sides separately.

- For patterns, cut with smooth long strokes but don't close the shears completely to the tip each time as this will cause a series of irregular edges. On the edge of the cutting line, mark notches by cutting around them.

Cut double notches should as one unit—you don't need to cut separate triangles.

TIP: It is better to cut the notches outward than inward as this leaves the full seam allowance in place.

Basting

Basting, also called tacking, is simply making temporary stitching to hold a trim or seam in place until you can permanently sew it.

You can use various basting approaches, including pin basting, but if you are working with complex shapes or are a beginner, you might want to use more secure basting methods.

Hand basting

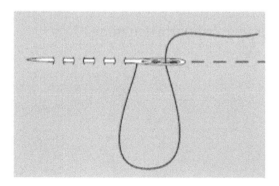

Hand basting involves basting with your hands by taking a needle with thread in and out of the fabric several times, forming a small stitch through all of the layers of fabric each time. You should pull the thread gently until tight but not so tight such that the fabric sticks out.

Machine basting

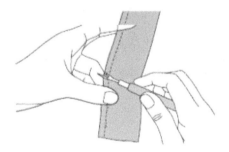

To machine-baste, set the stitch length to the highest possible setting and loosen the upper tension a bit—do not secure the seam's end by backstitching.

To make the basting simpler, cut through every 3rd or 4th stitch using a seam ripper when done.

Basting with tape

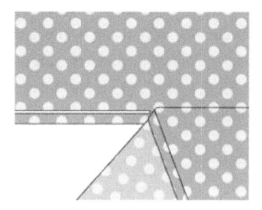

To baste with tape, use transparent, double-sided tape but don't stitch through it. This method is ideal for positioning trims and zippers before seeing. You can get water-soluble tapes that will disappear after the first wash to avoid the hassle of removing the tapes.

Basting with adhesive spray

Basting sprays are ideal when making quilts or when you need to hold large surfaces of the fabric. The spray can wash off easily, but ensure to follow the manufacturer's instructions and spray in a well-ventilated room.

Pressing

Pressing seams as you work on them is an important part of sewing, and if you do it right, it can help you achieve a crispy and professional look on your projects. You can also press to stretch or shrink the fabric, mark fold lines, fuse layers, or ease seam puckers.

Finger pressing

Some fabrics will allow you to press simple seams using your finger. All you have to do is use your thumb or finger to press down the seam allowance such that it lies down. You can run your fingernail down the seam to get a sharper crease but take caution not to stretch the fabric.

Pressing using an iron

Finger pressing only can't work on heavier fabrics (or complex seams); hence, you will need to press with an iron. Set the iron to the required temperature for the fabric—type—you are pressing and press down on the fabric with the seam facing up. You can press the seam open or flat to one side.

Pressing tips

- For delicate fabrics, wool and synthetics, use a pressing cloth to prevent burning/markings.

- Use the weight of the iron to press seams, and don't drag the iron along as you might stretch your piece out of shape.

- You need not press every seam after you finish it. Sew as much as possible, then press what you have done before proceeding.

- If you have used basting spray, fusible webbing, or basting tape on your project, use a soleplate or pressing cloth to prevent the adhesive from getting onto the iron's soleplate.

Working With the Needle and Thread

Ensure you are using the right thread and needle for the type of fabric you are working on.

If you are just getting started on your home machine, it is advisable to use a polyester, general-purpose sewing thread such as Coats & Clark- All Purpose, and a needle size 14.

Removing and replacing the needle

A screw clamp holds the needle in place; thus, it's really easy to take out without the need for special tools. To remove and replace the needle:

- A1 Bring up the presser foot and hold the needle between your thumb and finger. Turn the screw clamp counterclockwise to loosen the needle and slide out the needle at an angle.

- A2 Check first if the replacement needle is straight before fitting by placing it on a completely smooth and flat surface and holding it firmly at the shank. The gap in between the surface and the needle should be consistent all through.

- A3 With the presser foot still up, drive the end of the needle into the clamp and if the needle has a flat side, ensure it faced the same direction as the old needle. Clench the screw clam to make sure the needle stays in place.

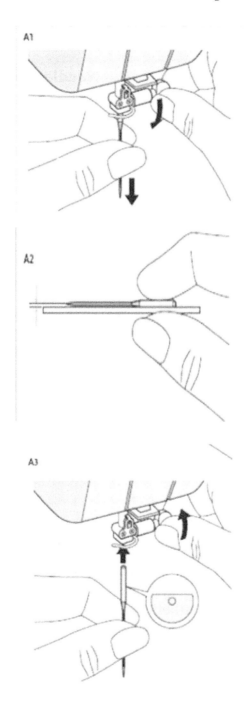

Use the following guide for the needle and thread:

Fabric type	Thread	Needle type	Needle size US/UK
Delicate- chiffon, tulle, organza, fine lace	Silk, fine mercerized cotton, fine synthetic thread	Microtex or sharp, universal	9/65
Medium weight- satin, vinyl, knits, deep pile fabrics, suiting, velvet, faille, chintz, pique, linen, gingham, percale, corduroy	Synthetic thread, medium mercerized cotton, silk, cotton	Universal	14/90
Medium-heavy- tweed, synthetic leather, denim, furnishing fabrics, sailcloth,	Cotton, synthetic thread, heavy-duty mercerized	Microtex or sharp, universal, denim	16/100

gabardine	cotton		
Lightweight- chiffon, velvet, silk, batiste, voile, taffeta, crêpe, organdie, jersey	Synthetic thread, medium mercerized cotton, silk	Microtex or sharp, universal	11/75
Heavy- heavy upholstery fabrics, over coatings, canvas	Cotton, synthetic thread, heavy-duty mercerized cotton	Denim	18/110
All weights- decorative hemming stitch, heirloom stitching	Silk, medium mercerized cotton, synthetic thread	Microtex or sharp, hemstitch	18/110
Medium and lightweight fabrics- decorative multi-needle	Medium mercerized cotton	Twin or triple	14/90

stitching			
All weights- decorative topstitching	Synthetic decorative thread or silk	Topstitching	16/100
Medium weight fabric- machine quilting	Silk, medium mercerized cotton, synthetic thread	Stippling or quilting	11/75 14/90
Stretch fabrics and synthetic knits- jersey, polyester, double knit, pannè velvet	Silk, medium mercerized cotton, synthetic thread	Stretch or ballpoint	14/90 11/75
Leather- kidskin, suede	Silk, medium mercerized cotton, synthetic thread	Leather	11/75 14/90 16/100
Medium and lightweight	Synthetic or silk	Spring or embroidery	14/90

fabrics- machine embroidery	decorative thread		16/100
Medium weight fabric- free-motion machine quilting	Silk, medium mercerized cotton, synthetic thread	Spring	14/90

Section 4

Getting Started With Sewing: Step-by-Step

As we have already established, the number and type of stitches you get to sew entirely depends on your machine. Some machines have a large number of stitches, while others just have a few basic ones. You might find that you won't use some stitches as often as others.

The procedure for sewing the different stitches is more or less the same—find the procedure in the next sub-topic)- it's just a matter of changing the stitch pattern on the pattern selector dial.

Winding The Bobbin

Before stitching, you must first wind your thread onto the bobbin. If you have the manufacturer's manual, then follow those instructions for your machine model. If you don't have the manual, you can wind the bobbin as follows:

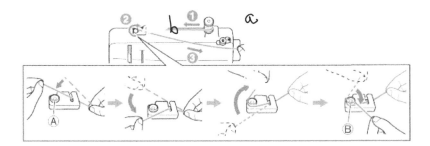

- Position an empty bobbin to the rod of the bobbin winder. Never do winding on a bobbin that already contains some thread; you will end up with thread knots and tension problems. If the bobbin has some thread, remove it first.

- First, disengage the bobbin winding clutch—when disengaged, the needle bar won't move with a turn on the hand wheel. You can use the motor to wind the bobbin without the machine vibrating as it is running.

- On newer machines, release the clutch by moving the bobbin towards the bobbin winding stop. If your bobbin winding clutch is at the center of the hand wheel, turn the knob counterclockwise as you restrict the hand wheel from moving.

- Add the thread spool on the suitable spool pin; it can be the same as that used for sewing—although other machines have a separate one specifically for bobbin winding.

- Remove the thread from the thread spool and pass it through any thread guides that are on your way to the bobbin winding tension disks (remember these disks are not the same as the main tension disks; these are much smaller). After passing the thread through the disks, continue passing the thread to the rest of the thread guides (if any) and then to the bobbin.

- Move the thread through one of the slots or holes in the bobbin's side and hold it as you begin winding the bobbin. You will let go of the thread after you've wound a few turns.

- Place pressure on the foot pedal to start turning the bobbin. It should wind evenly, and if it doesn't, you need to figure out why before proceeding. You can guide the thread using your fingers to ensure it winds evenly.

- Avoid winding too much thread on the bobbin because it will interfere with tension or cause thread breakage since the extra thread will make contact with the bobbin case and prevent the bobbin from turning freely in its case. See the pic below for a properly wound bobbin:

Overfilled   *Properly filled*

- Remember to re-engage the clutch once done.

Now that you already know how to wind your bobbin, here are the essential stitches you will use often:

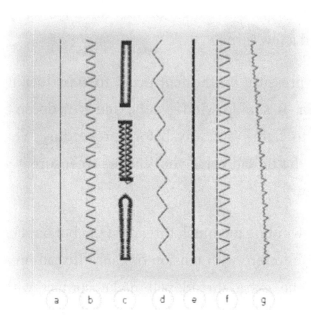

1: A straight stitch

This stitch is the main sewing stitch used in around 99% of sewing. The stitch works for hems, seams, mending, and topstitching. However, this stitch does not stretch, making it not ideal for stretch knits.

2: Zigzag

You can use this stitch as a satin stitch for sewing on stitch monograms and appliques, finishing seam allowance to ensure that fabric edges do not fray, sewing stretch knits and buttons, and decoratively.

3: Buttonhole

The buttonhole stitch is a box composed of small zigzag stitches. You can stitch a buttonhole using a zigzag stitch, but it is more convenient to use a buttonhole stitch. Computerized machines offer an automatic 1 step buttonhole, while mechanical machines offer a 4 step buttonhole.

4: Tricot/elastic stitch

Also known as a 3 step zigzag, you can use this stitch to stitch on knit and elastic fabrics. The stitches are a bit smaller than the zigzag, reducing the chances of snagging—the stitch has lots of stretches.

5: Stretch straight

A stretch straight is made by making one stitch forward and one back, then one forward. This stitch is very durable as it runs on one spot three times, making the stitch ideal for high-stress seams.

You can also use the stitch for knits as the stitch has a built-in stretch (the feed dog stretches your fabric a bit).

6: Overcasting

This stitch utilizes both straight and zigzag stitches. You will use this stitch to tuck in the raw edges of the fabric to avoid fraying.

7: Blind hem

A blind hem sews several small zigzags and then a large zigzag. The stitch is usually used for hemming and is invisible from the other side.

How to Stitch

If you are new to sewing, you will need to spend some time getting used to stitching before starting an actual project. To stitch, follow the following process:

- **Begin stitching:** Ensure you have pulled the bobbin threads and the needle under and behind, or sideways, of the raised presser foot. Have your fabric under the presser foot such that it mostly lies on the left of the presser foot. Press the needle down button or turn the hand wheel to lower the needle into your fabric. Begin stitching after lowering the presser foot- start slow.

- **Use the screw-on magnetic guide:** This is a cloth guide made to attach to the needle plate. You can adjust it to fit the correct distance from the needle. As you begin stitching, align this guide with the edge of your fabric.

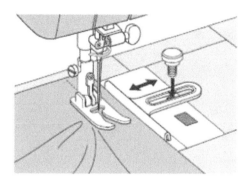

- **Position your hands:** As you go on stitching, have your hands on either side of the needle so that you can easily guide the fabric through the machine.

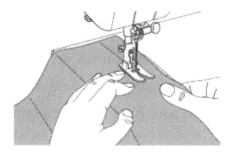

- **Control the pace:** With an electric machine, a knee bar or a foot pedal controls your stitching speed. The more you push, the faster the machine goes, so be sure to push it slowly at the beginning, just to get it going.

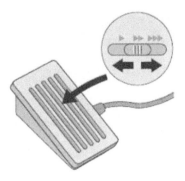

Most modern machines have a speed controller, a separate slider, that you can set to limit your maximum speed.

- **Guide the fabric through the machine:** Keeping the bulk of the material on the left side of the needle, use your hands to steer the fabric in the right direction. Do not push or pull the fabric to move it through the machine; the feed dog will move it at the required pace to match the needle.

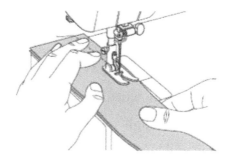

- **Curving a corner:** To achieve a neat stitch where you need to make a corner, follow the following steps:

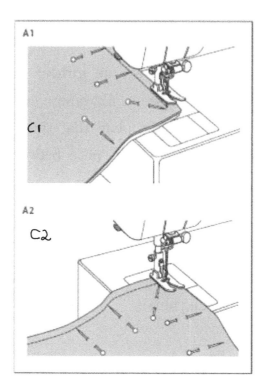

- C1- Stitch up to the exact point where you want to start turning a corner and leave your needle in the fabric and lift the presser foot.

- C2- rotate your work on the needle, ensuring you are careful enough not to pull on the needle such that you will now be stitching in an entirely new direction (the direction should align with your corner).

- C3- Lower the pressure foot and continue stitching.

- **Use a seam allowance guide:** You will need to make sure your seam allowances are even. Look for lines on the needle plate that show common seam allowances—this is the space between the stitching line and the edge of the fabric.

  Usually, the seam allowance is 12mm (½ inches), 15mm (5/8 inches), or 6mm (¼ inch). If your project needs an unusual seam allowance, you can mark this using masking tape.

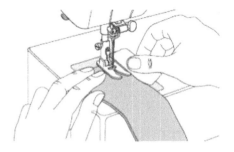

- **Secure the thread ends:** Reinforcing your stitch at the end of the seam prevents the threads from coming loose—you can do this at the beginning of a stitch by reverse stitching on the sewing machine—known as a backstitch.

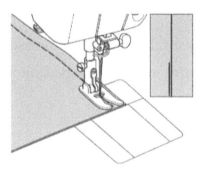

To reverse stitch, start at around 12mm (1/2 inch) from where you began stitching, stitch in reverse back to the edge, and then stitch again forward normally. To complete your stitch, finish by stitching in reverse along the stitch line for 12mm (1/2 inch).

- **Cut thread:** If your machine has an automatic thread cutter, press the button to cut the thread at the end of the seam. When you've done this, raise the presser foot and take out your fabric.

Stitching With Older Mechanical Machines

There is a difference between sewing with older machines and new computerized or electrical machines. For example, while you can set the stitch type on the computerized machines, you cannot do the same with older mechanical machines.

To stitch with an older machine, follow the following steps:

- Place your fabric under the presser foot just at the spot where you want to begin stitching and lower the presser foot.

- Grab the thread tails using your left hand's fingers and pull the tails towards the back of your machine—don't pull too hard such that the needle bends or you pull out more thread; pull just enough to prevent the tails from being pulled into the machine as you begin sewing. If the thread tails have pulled into the needle hole at the beginning of sewing, most mechanical machines will form an unpleasant knot of thread at the bottom of your fabric.

- Use your right-hand fingers to guide the fabric through the machine—have the fabric about 2 inches in front of the presser foot.

- Use your foot to press on the foot pedal to get the machine going.

- After you've made a few stitches, you can now let go of the thread tails so that you can free your hand to assist in guiding the fabric through the presser foot.

- Let the machine move the fabric, do not push or pull on it. Your effort should only be guiding the fabric in the sewing direction.

    NOTE: However, you might need to help the machine move the fabric when sewing a thick seam. In this case, you will use the hand wheel to advance the machine one stitch at a time. Ensure that you only move the fabric to the next stitch position when the needle is up.

- When you've finished sewing, rotate the needle past the highest point using the hand wheel and then move it down a bit before you raise the presser foot to remove the fabric. This step is necessary to make the thread disengage from the hook mechanism of the sewing machine.

- As you remove the fabric, pull it towards the rear of the machine and cut the hanging thread leaving only around 4 inches from the bobbin and needle, leaving your machine ready for more sewing.

Section 5

Sewing Seams

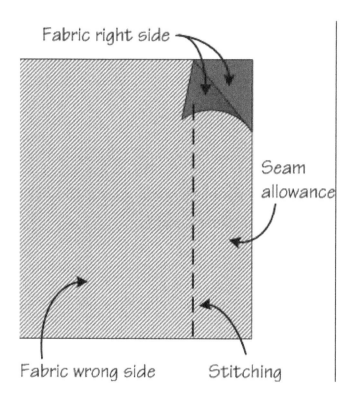

Plain seam parts

Joining pieces of fabric together forms the basic construction method for any project. A well-sewn seam should be almost invisible. To do this, you will need to reduce seam bulk and neaten your seam allowance.

You can create different types of seams, with a straight seam being the most commonly used.

Straight Seams

Types of straight seams include:

1: *Plain seam*

A plain seam is the simplest seams meant to hold together two or more layers of fabric together.

To create this seam:

- S1 Secure your pieces of fabric with pins right side together, ensuring to align the raw edges.

- S2 Use a straight stitch on your machine to sew the seam with a bit of backstitching at all ends to secure the seam.

- S3 Remove any pins and basting threads and press the seam.

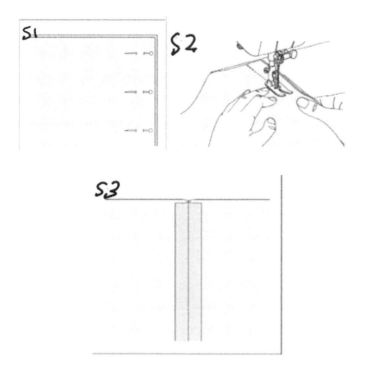

2: Intersecting seams

Sometimes you might need to join two seamed sections. To do this, follow the following steps:

- S1 On each section, press the seams open. Cut the ends of the seam allowances for original seams to reduce bulk.

- S2 Have the sections right side together and match the seams exactly such that they will run across the new seam you've sewn at a right angle. Baste or pin along your new seam to hold the alignment as you continue sewing.

- S3 Press the new seam open.

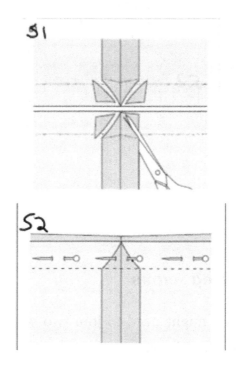

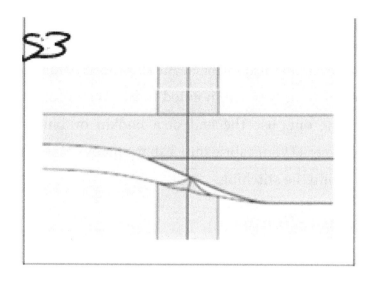

3: Grading seams

When working with several layers or thicker fabrics, your seams might get bulky and not lie flat and smooth. To get rid of this bulk, trim down the seam allowances such that each has a different width, which we call grading.

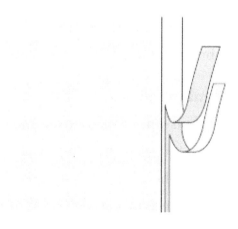

Points and corners

Cut off excess fabric in the seam allowance before turning a corner to get a neat and pointed finish. When turning to the right side out, use the end of a bodkin or blunt knitting needle to ease your fabric into a sharp point—take care not to push it into the stitching.

Finishing Seams

There are many ways to finish off a seam and leave it looking neat and professional. You can stitch your seam and then trim the raw edges with pinking shears; you can also double stitch by making another stitch next to the first. You can also be creative and zigzag stitch along the raw edge—or bias bind by enclosing the raw edges in a folded strip.

Lapped Seam

These seams are usually used for interlining and interfacing and for thick fabrics that don't fray, e.g., leather.

- **For the main fabrics:** Have the seam lines in line at the center and lap the edges over one another. Make a stitch along the seam line to join and trim the seam allowance of the piece on top close to the stitching line. Make a second parallel stitch to hold the seam allowance of the piece on the bottom.

- **For interlining and interfacing:** Have the seam lines in line at the center and lap the edges over one another. Make a stitch along the seam line to join.

Enclosed Seam

These don't require finishing at the raw edges since the edges are closed as you make the seam. Types of enclosed seams include:

1: Self-bound Seam

Such seams have one edge of the seam allowance folded over to encase the other edge. This seam is great with sheer fabrics that would otherwise show the seam allowance right through. To make this seam:

- S1 Make a plain seam and trim one side of the seam allowance to 3mm (1/8 inch).

- S2 Turn the edge of the other seam allowance by 3mm (1/8 inch) near the seam's inside and press. Turn the pressed edge over again to cover the raw edge of the seam allowance. Have the folded edge over the original seam line.

- S3 Stitch near the folded edge through the layers of the seam allowance. Press seam allowance to one side.

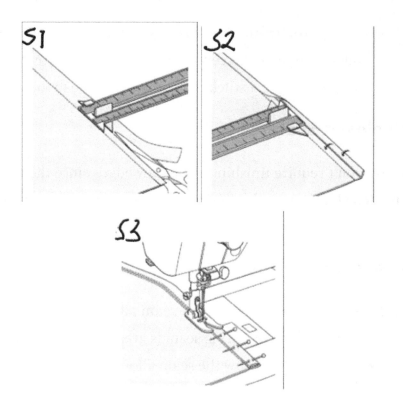

2: French seam

This seam is great for delicate fabrics, but you can't use it on a curved edge. To make this seam:

- S1 Have the wrong sides together and stitch the seam 9mm (3/8 inches) from the edge. Clip seam allowance to 3mm (⅛ inch) and press it open.

- S2 Enfold the fabric along the stitching line with the right sides together. Pin and make a second seam on the seam line.

- S3 Make sure no threads are protruding from the raw edges—trim and press flat.

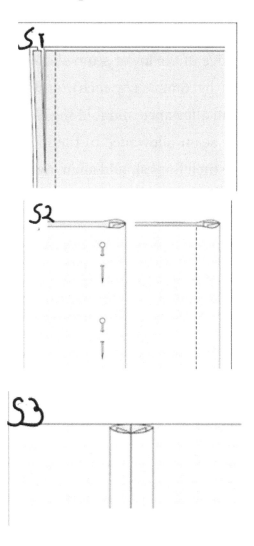

3: Mock french seam

You can make this seam in a curved edge. The steps for the seam are:

- S1 Have the right sides facing each other and stitch a plain seam. Trim to 12mm (1/2 inch).

- S2 Take the upper seam allowance, press it back flat, fold the edge of the lower seam allowance towards the seam line by 6mm (1/4 inch), and press. Take the lower seam allowance and fold the same way and turn the upper seam allowance to the lower one- the fold lines and stitch lines should align. Again press.

- S3 Make a stitch to bring the seam allowances together.

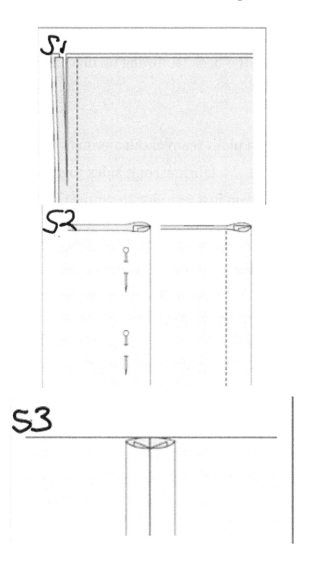

4: Flat-fell seam

This seam is best for heavy-duty fabric prone to wear— usually used for jeans. To get that decorative effect, you can work the double line of stitching with contrast threads. There is also a welt seam used on such heavy materials but is less bulky, thanks to the back trimming on one edge.

For this stitch:

- S1 Make a plain seam about 15mm (5/8 inch) from the edge with the fabric wrong sides together. Trim seam allowance on just one side to 3mm (1/8 inch).

- S2 Flatten the seam and turn under 6mm (1/4 inch) through the edge of the untrimmed seam allowance. Fold this over such that it is covering the edge you trimmed. Baste or pin.

- S3 Make an edgestitch along the fold, keeping it parallel to the seam line.

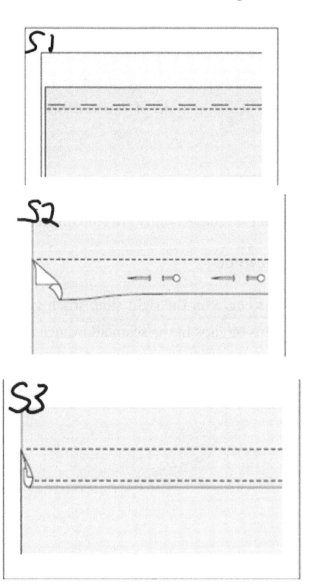

Shaped Seams

These seams are similar to the plain seams but usually clipped or notched to get rid of excess fabric such that the seam lies flat.

Curved Seams

These can either be convex (outward) or concave (inward).

1: Concave curve

To achieve this curve on the right side, stitch your seam and make little snips or clips in the seam allowance up to near the line of stitching—but not through it. Make them evenly space.

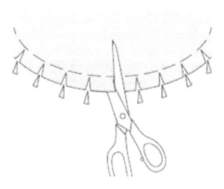

2: Convex curve

To get this curve on the right side, stitch your seam and cut wedge-shaped notches from the seam allowance to eliminate the excess fullness. Try and keep the notches fairly narrow to avoid a jagged look.

Princess Seam

You will use this seam when you need to stitch a concave edge to a convex edge. To make this seam:

- S1 Make a stay stitch inside the seam line of the concave piece and make small snips in the seam allowance at regular intervals along the concave curve.

- S2 Have the clipped piece on top and pin the right sides together. Pair the markings and spread the snips of the concave edge as needed to fit those of the convex edge. Set your machine to a shorter stitch length than normal and sew your stitch.

- S3 Make small snips at regular intervals along the convex edge—be careful not to cut through the stitching.

- S4 Smooth the seam from one side first and then from the other and press it open over the curved shape.

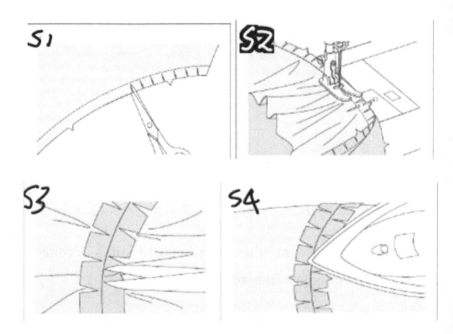

Darts

You can use these to add fullness to allow for body curves such as bust, shoulders, hips, and waist. They can either be single or double darts.

1: Single dart

This dart comes in from the seam line, and its widest point will be at the seam. For this seam:

- S1 Double over the fabric in half with the right sides together and sew from seam line to point, and have a few stitches beyond. Don't backstitch.

- S2 finish your seam with long ends, tie and snip short-press moving towards the center.

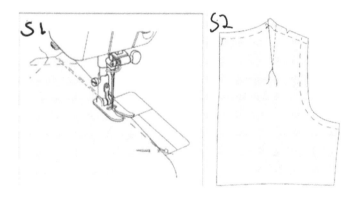

2: Double pointed dart

These are usually positioned away from the seam and run vertically.

- S1 If your dart seems very deep at the center, take out the triangle of fabric at the center and clean-cut each end near the seam, taking care not to cut through the stitching.

- S2 After you cut, use the iron tip to press the dart such that it lies flat to the garment working each end at a time.

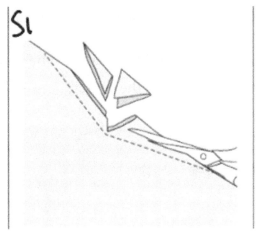

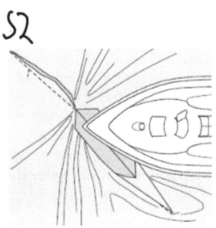

Section 6

Buttonholes and
Zippers

The chances are high that whatever you are working on will need some closure. The closure can either be functional or decorative. The most common types of closure are zippers and buttonholes, which even the most basic sewing machine can sew.

Zippers

The thought of installing a zipper might feel intimidating, but this section will give you everything you need to know on installing one—perfectly.

How to shorten a zipper

Before we discuss how to install zippers, let's focus on shortening a zipper when you don't get the exact length you want—you can also use continuous zippers that you can cut as needed.

Shortening a closed-end zipper

Make a new bottom stop stitch several times across the teeth (use a strong thread). Conceal the excess teeth within the seam or cut them off.

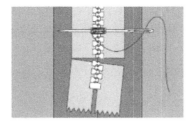

<u>Shortening a separating zipper</u>

As you measure the zipper position, have it such that the excess is at the top end. Once in place, cut the excess zipper and conceal the ends within the waistband, facing or collar.

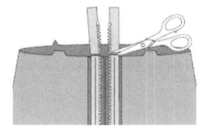

Using a zipper foot

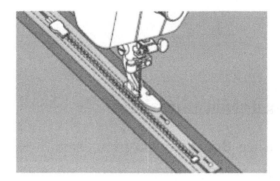

You will need a zipper foot to install zippers. A zipper foot is a narrow piece of metal featuring a notch at the sides to allow the needle to move up and down. Its narrow shape moves along the zipper teeth and allows you to make stitches close to them.

You have to set the needle to come down to the right or left of the foot (not center). To achieve this, move the foot side to side on an adjustable slide and set it such that the needle comes down adjacent to the zipper teeth.

Centered zipper

A centered zipper is usually placed at the center back or center front of a garment. To insert this zipper:

- Z1 Measure and mark the position of the zipper on the seam. Use the zipper as the guide and leave enough room at the top for making a facing seam. Stitch the seam up to the mark indicating the beginning of the zipper and zigzag the edges of the seam allowance.

- Z2 Place the zipper, while closed, over the wrong side of the seam and pin and baste in position. Turn fabric to the right side.

- Z3 Begin at the top and stitch down the zipper, across the bottom, and then to the top. If necessary, move the zipper slider to keep the seam straight.

- Z4 Add the waistband or facing to the fabric and slipstitch the ends. Ensure no facings or stitches can catch the zipper while it is in use. Take out the bastings.

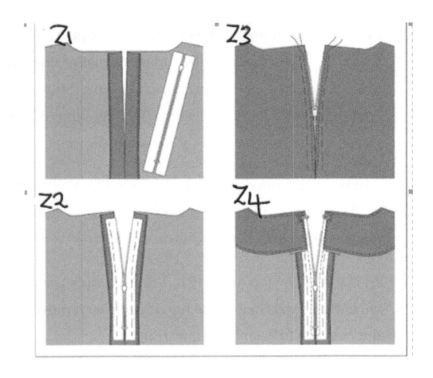

Lapped zipper

This zipper is set such that one side of its opening conceals the zipper teeth- only a single line of stitching shows on the right side of the fabric, making it less conspicuous.

To insert the zipper:

- Z1 Mark the zipper opening on the fabric and place the right sides together. Stitch up to the bottom mark and backstitch to secure. Zigzag the seam allowance edges and baste.

- Z2 Have the fabric flat and fold the top of the seam allowance back— leave the bottom extending outward and lying flat. Have the zipper face down on seam allowance with teeth over the seamline. Baste along the seam allowance around 6mm (1/4inch) from the zipper teeth.

- Z3 flip the zipper face up along the basting line and fold under the elongated seam allowance. Stitch close to the edge of the fold in the bottom seam allowance.

- Z4 Turn the garment to the right side and have the seam allowances opened flat underneath, and baste the zipper to the garment up the unsewn side and across the end. Have the needle to the left of the zipper foot and topstitch all around. Get rid of the basting.

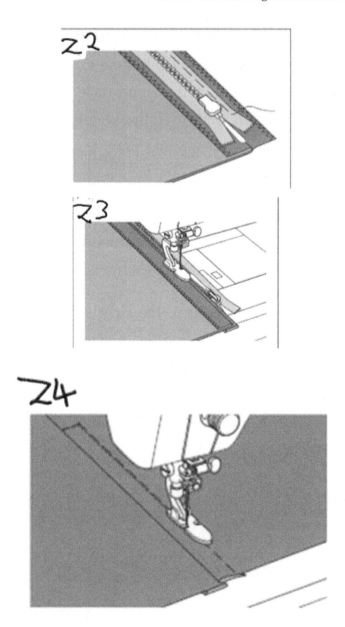

Concealed zipper

A concealed zipper appears as a continuous seam, giving a clean finish to garments. Some machines do have a rolling zipper foot for installing these zippers, but this method works even if you have a regular zipper foot.

- Z1 Mark the position of the zipper on the fabrics, open the zipper and place it face down on the right side of a piece of the fabric—the coils should run along the position of the seam line and the tape should lie on the seam allowance. Baste or pin.

- Z2 Start by uncurling the coil at the upper edge to make it feed in the groove as shown below and stitch to the slider. If you are using a regular zipper foot, uncurl and place the foot so that the needle comes down on the right side where you stitch as close as you can to the coils. Reinforce by backstitching.

- Z3 Baste or pin the zippers' other half on the other piece of fabric, ensuring the lower edge of the fabric is aligned well. Uncurl and feed on the rolling zipper foot (move to the left side of the needle if using a regular zipper foot). Stitch in place.

- Z4 Close the zipper and see if it is invisible on the right side of the garment. For the seam allowance below the zipper, baste them together and switch to a regular zipper foot if using a rolling zipper foot. Pull out the zipper tape and finish stitching the seam.

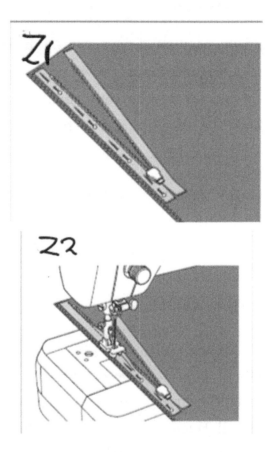

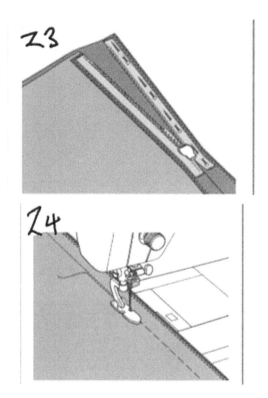

Separating zipper

When unfastened, this zipper separated apart. To insert:

- Z1 Baste edges of zipper opening close and press open the seam allowances. Have the zipper at the center of seam allowances face down and closed, have the hemline and the bottom stop aligned.

- Z2 Work from the right side and stitch along the zipper sides—have them parallel to the basted seam and about 3mm (1/8 inch) away). Pull the ends through the wrong side and fasten (don't backstitch).

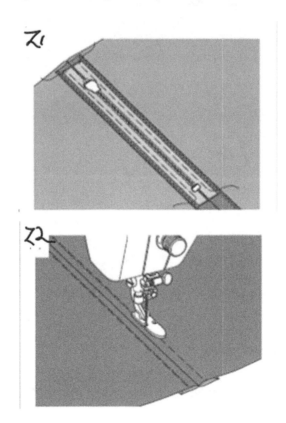

Buttonholes

Many modern machines have an automatic buttonhole function. If you intend to sew many of them, investing in a machine with several buttonhole designs is a good idea.

Placing buttonholes

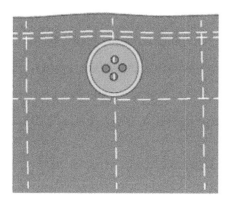

Vertical buttonholes should be on the centerline, and the top end should be 3mm (1/8 inch) above the position of the button. On the other hand, horizontal buttonholes should drag out 3mm (1/8 inch) over the center line and towards the edge of the attire.

For both cases, the actual button should attach to the centerline but make sure there is at least 6mm (1/4 inch) of fabric between the edge of the garment and the edge of the button.

Normally, buttonholes are placed on the left front for men's pieces and on the right front for women's pieces.

4-step machine buttonhole

You can stitch this buttonhole on machines with two settings for the buttonhole. It's called 4-step because you have to switch between the two settings two times. For this buttonhole:

- B1 Using the buttonhole foot, straight stitch on each line of the buttonhole opening to stabilize the edge. Set machine to zigzag with short width and length and stitch along just one long side of the buttonhole.

- B2 Have the needle down and raise the foot, turn your fabric 180 degrees and adjust the width of the stitch so that you can make some long stitches across the width of the buttonhole to stabilize the end. Do the same to the other side and end.

- B3 Turn the stitch width to 0 and make some stitches to secure the thread end and pull them to the back. Trim close. Slit the buttonhole open using a seam ripper at the centerline.

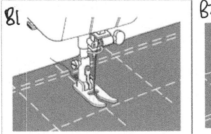 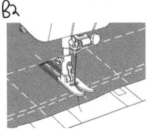

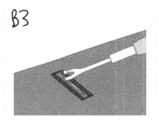

1-step buttonhole

Some more expensive machines have a function for a 1-step buttonhole where you place the button in a holder on the machine to set the buttonhole size. The buttonhole is then stitched automatically to fit the button.

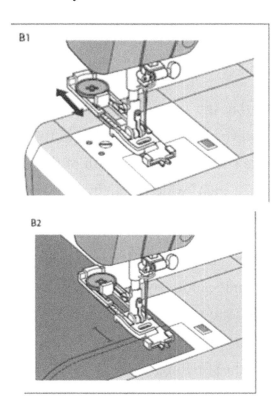

Bound buttonhole

This buttonhole doesn't have zigzag stitching around its opening; rather, a separate piece of fabric bound around it neatens it. To make the binding, match the fabric to make it as inconspicuous as possible—but you can have it in contrast to get a decorative effect. For this buttonhole:

- B1 Cut about 2.5cm (1 inch) of the main fabric longer and wider than the buttonhole. Place it at the center of the buttonhole, right sides together, and mark the buttonhole ends and centerline on it. Baste 3mm (1/8 inch) from the centerline of the buttonhole along each side.

- B2 Overlay the patch's sides to the center along the lines you've basted and baste again to secure the laps. Machine stitch along the length of the buttonhole and 6mm (1/4 inch) wide through all layers following the buttonhole marks.

- B3 Overlay the buttonhole area of the garment in half across and cautiously cut along the center of the buttonhole to not beyond 3mm (1/8 inch) of the end. Cut diagonally into all corners taking care not to cut through the stitching.

- B4 Push the patch of fabric to the wrong sides of the garment and press flat. Hold the lips together with a slipstitch along the folds. Square the opening by pulling gently on the small triangles on the wrong side, then stitch across to hold in place.

- B5 For the buttonhole slit, overlay facing to one side and use a sharp pair of scissors to slit a buttonhole, ensuring to stop 6mm (1/4 inch) away from the end. Align the slit with the buttonhole, pull back and overlay raw edges, pin then, hand stitch the facing to the patch of the buttonhole.

- B6 Take out the basting holding the edges closed.

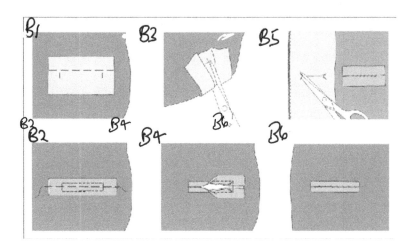

Eyelet buttonhole

This buttonhole is circular, and thus, you can use it for decoration, military-style buttons, and even to make great belt holes. If your machine has a variety of buttonhole functions, it probably has an eyelet one too.

For an eyelet, simply use an embroidery or satin foot on your machine, mark the center of the eyelet position on the right side of the fabric and stitch around with the automatic eyelet function.

Alternatively, you can set the stitch to zigzag with short width and length, cover or drop the feed dog and stitch slowly around the mark of the eyelet in a circle. Use a fabric punch to punch out the center or use sharp pointed scissors.

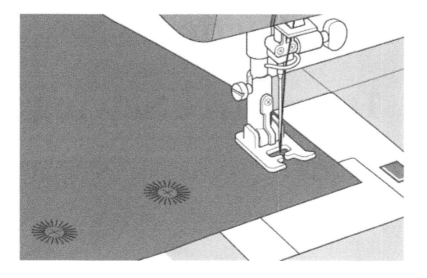

Section 7

Decorative Sewing

Decorative sewing techniques make your work unique and pleasant to look at. Your machine can create beautiful, decorative sewn work or add decorative touches to already finished work. You can do this using appliques, embroidery, and decorative stitches.

Appliqué

Appliqué revolves around utilizing fabric patches to decorate the base fabric; it can also be used for decoration or to hide stains and holes. To add on an appliqué, you'll need:

- Hand needle

- Iron and ironing board

- Lightweight fusible interfacing

- Appliqué, satin-stitch, or open-toe foot

- Fabric marker or tailor's chalk

- Basting spray or pins

- Scissors

- Fabric for the appliqué

Procedure

based on the manufacturer's instructions on iron time and temperature, put fusible interfacing on the wrong side of the applique fabric. Use chalk or fabric marker to draw the shape of the applique on the wrong side of the fabric

Cut the appliqué out and place it on the fabric. Baste or pin in place.

Select the appliqué or satin stitch on the machine and select zigzag with a length of 1mm and width of 4 mm.

Turn the hand wheel to get the needle to the right side of the zigzag and place the fabric in line with the needle such that it comes on the exterior of the applique.

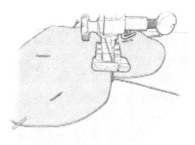

Satin-stitch all around the appliqué and leave long thread tails at the end and the begging rather than backstitching.

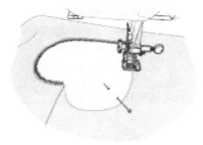

Pull the top thread tails using a hand sewing needle and pass them through the wrong side of the fabric. Hand tie off.

TIP: You can still add appliqué with other decorative stitches; for instance, reverse applique stitches or blanket stitches.

Decorative Stitches

Many sewing machines now have several decorative stitches such as zigzag, embroidery, triple zigzag, cross-stitch, and smocking. What you can do is experiment with different lengths and widths to achieve the look you desire.

What you will need here includes:

- Iron and ironing board

- Satin-stitch or open-toe foot

- Wash-away or tear-away stabilizer

- Decorative thread (variegated, metallic, rayon, or embroidery)

- Embroidery needle or metallic needle

- Quilting bar

Procedure

Have the stabilizer on the wrong side of the fabric- as per the manufacturer's instructions. Chose a decorative stitch and set the width and length as needed.

Position the open toe foot or satin stitch and place the quilting bar into the shank.

Sew a row of decorative stitches across the whole length of the fabric, select another type of stitch, align the quilt bar on the stitch you just created and stitch the other row.

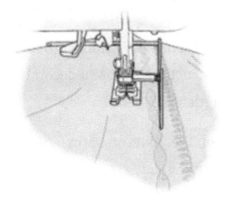

Keep doing this until you achieve your desired look. When done, remove the stabilizer as per the manufactures' recommendations.

TIP: You can use an all-purpose thread to create decorative stitching, or you could experiment with some intricate threads such as metallic threads, glow in the dark, or variegated threads.

Monograms

You can make this using complex scripts or basic block letters. To make a monogram, you will need the following tools:

- Hand sewing needle

- Fabric marker

- Iron and ironing board

- Free-motion embroidery foot

- Darning plate (optional)

- Wash-away stabilizer

- Decorative thread (embroidery, metallic, variegated, or rayon)

- Embroidery hoop

- Embroidery needle or metallic needle

- Letter template

Procedure

Design your monogram. You can use your computer to print out a letter or use an already created template.

Use a fabric marker to trace the letter on a layer of stabilizer.

Place the letter in between 2 layers of stabilizer, ensuring an even stretching and that it is tight—have the stabilizer with the letter on top.

Place the hooped fabric under the foot- push it up on the presser foot to get extra high clearance.

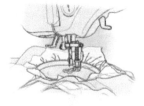

Have the free motion embroidery foot installed and align the bar with the top needle bar—install the metallic or embroidery needle. Lower the feed dog, set the machine to a wide zigzag, and begin stitching.

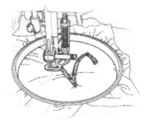

You will need to use your hands to move the hoop as you sew.

Leave behind long thread tails and use a hand needle to pull the top threads through the wrong side of the fabric; hand-tie them off. Take out the stabilizer as per the manufacturer's recommendations.

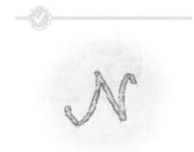

TIP: Block letters are the easiest to create; practice with them fast before trying fancier script letters.

Check your machine for a stitch regulator that times the stitch with the hoop's movement to ensure the stitches remain even all through.

Free-motion Embroidery

Free-motion embroidery is an excellent way to add embellishment to garments. You can be as creative as you want by either drawing out a design and stitching with it or designing as you sew—it is more like 'thread painting. The tools needed here include:

- Hand sewing needle

- Embroidery hoop

- Tailor's chalk, transfer paper, or fabric marker

- Wash-away or tear-away stabilizer

- Darning plate/the ability to lower the feed dog

Procedure

Apply the stabilizer (on the wrong side) as per the manufacturer's instructions.

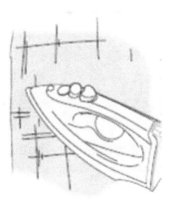

Use the transfer paper, marker, or chalk to draw the design on the right side of the fabric.

Have the free motion embroidery in place, ensuring that the needle bar is right below the bar.

Cover the feed dog with a darning plate or lower it instead.

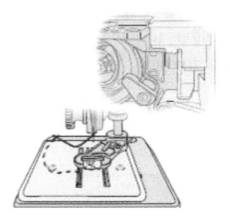

Hoop the fabric, ensuring that it is taut and evenly stretched out.

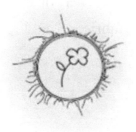

Place the hooped fabric under the foot—push it up on the presser foot to get extra high clearance. You will need to use your hands to move the hoop as you sew.

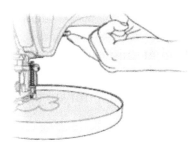

Leave behind long thread tails and use a hand needle to pull the top threads through the wrong side of the fabric. Hand-tie them off. Take out the stabilizer as per the manufacturer's recommendations.

TIP: You can thread trace on the fabric to outline motifs using a straight stitch.

Patchwork and Piecing

This process involves sewing together small bits of fabric to come up with a larger block of fabric. Here, you must be very accurate to ensure that the larger block is your desired size—the 6mm (1/4 inch) foot ensures this.

The tools you will need here include:

- Rotary cutter, mat, and quilt ruler

- All-purpose thread and a universal needle

- ¼" (6 mm) foot

- Scissors

- Paper and pen

- Pins

- Iron and ironing board

Procedure

First, decide the size of your placemat and draw this on a piece of paper—this is a 46 by 30 cm (18 by 12 inches) rectangle.

Draw lines that will divide the rectangle into simple blocks— here, there are lines every 8cm (3 inches), making 24 squares.

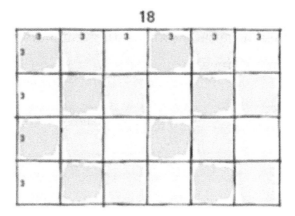

Measure the sides of the blocks and increase by 1.3cm (1/2 inch) on each block for the seam allowance to account for the 6mm (1/4 inch) seam allowance on each side.

Use a mat, quilt ruler, and a rotary cutter to cut out the fabrics as desired.

Pile up the fabrics for each row in the order that you will sew them.

Secure the 6mm (1/4 inch) foot on the machine and select straight stitch, have the needle at the center with the length being 2.5mm (1/8 inch).

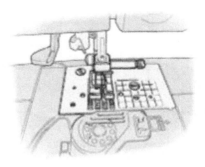

Stitch together the first pieces and have the raw edges right against the foot's guide.

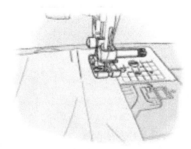

Keep stitching all the squares for the first row and then press the seam allowances to one side.

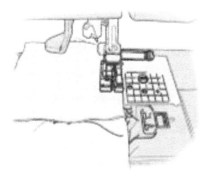

Stitch the blocks for the rest of the row and press the seam allowances. Finish your work by stitching together all the rows with a 6mm (1/4 inch) seam allowance.

TIP(S): If you are sewing together many pieces of fabric, continuous sewing can be a great time saver.

Once you are at the end of one seam, stitch one stitch off the edge and stitch right to the next part without lifting the presser foot. Keep stitching on as many pieces as you need, and once done, cut the chain to break apart the sections. Press the seam allowances.

Pearls and Beading

Adding beads and pearls to clothes used to be tedious as they needed gluing on or hand-sewing into the fabric. But now, a beading foot makes this task much easier and gives perfect results.

For this procedure, you will need:

- Invisible or matching all-purpose thread

- Fabric marker or tailor's chalk

- Pearl and beading foot

- Ruler

Procedure

Use a chalk/marker and a ruler to mark placement for the trim.

Secure a beading and pearling foot on your machine and set it to wide zigzag with a length of 3mm.

Place the fabric under the foot and have the guideline under the grove. Add your bead to the grove and lower the foot.

Walk the machine to make some stitches using the hand wheel, ensuring the needle doesn't come in contact with the bead-adjust width if need be.

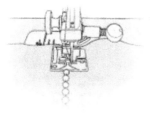

Stitch trim in place and secure by backstitching on both ends.

Section 8

Basic Sewing Projects for Beginners

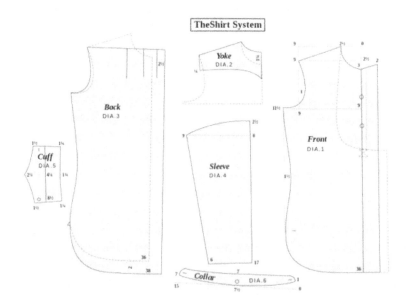

1: Zipper Pouch

Supplies

- 7-inch zipper

- Small amounts of 2 fabrics (you can use scraps)

Procedure

Cut 2 pieces each of different fabric to get a total of 4 pieces; each of the pieces should be around 7.5 inches wide and 5.5 inches tall.

You can either add ruffles to the fabric or leave it as it is. If you do, sew it on where you want it on a fabric meant for the outer piece.

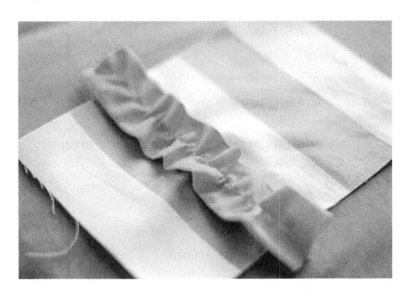

Start putting your bag together by taking one of the outer piece fabric and one inner piece and placing them together with their right sides facing each other. The zipper should get sandwiched between them along the edge at the top, and its right side should touch the right side of the outer fabric.

Make a straight stitch—or use any other stitch of choice—along the top and into the layers of fabric with the zipper between them. Move the zipper away to allow you to sew perfectly.

It should look like this when done.

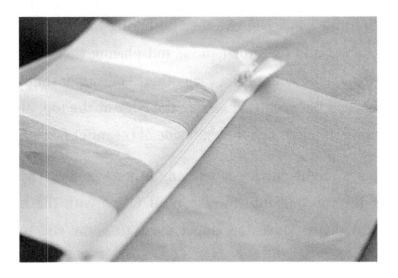

Now do the same with the other two fabrics and the other side of the zipper. If you had ruffles, you should sew right through them, with the excess hanging off. Cut this off only when done with this step.

You should have something like this now:

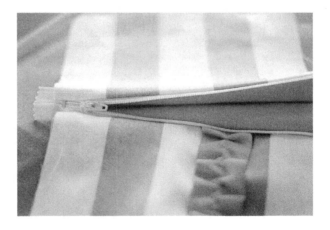

Press your work nice and flat.

Topstitch along both sides of the zipper and open it most of the way. Fold your bag such that the fabrics touch with the right sides together—the inner pieces should be touching each other, and the outer pieces should also be touching.

Sew all around all pieces leaving only a small opening for turning when sewing the inner part:

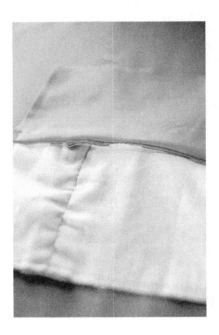

Trim the excess ruffle or zipper and turn it right side out. Make the corners crisp by poking them out. Stitch shut the opening, press again, and you voila! You've made a zipper pouch!

2: Christmas Napkin Rings

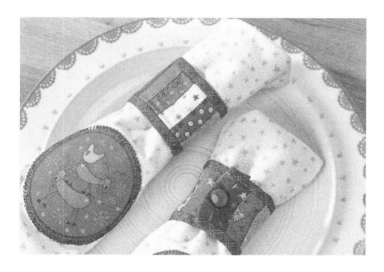

Supplies

- Velcro (Or press studs)

- Interfacing (8 inches x 10 inches)

- Fabric (Twelve (12) assorted 1-inch x 10-inch fabric strips)

- Backing fabric (13 inches x 7 inches)

Procedure

Sew the 12 strips of fabric together along the long edges using a 1/4 inch seam and press the seams in one direction.

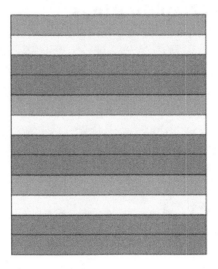

Evenly cut the strips you've pieced together into 4 2-inch strips and iron interface onto the wrong sides of one another.

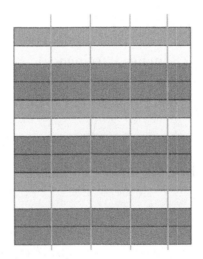

With the right sides together, place a pieced strip on top of the backing. The backing will be larger than the strip, so ensure to line up the raw edges and sew along the long aides and one short end.

Use the open end to turn the napkin ring inside out and press flat- the backing will create a border edge on each side of the patchwork. Use a scrap of backing fabric to bind or turn the end in and close with a slip stitch.

Press the studs in each end or attach the Velcro. Repeat this to create 4 napkin rings.

Customizing your napkins

You can add a special touch to your napkins using applique and special motifs to customize plain napkins.

Procedure

Cut out 4 17.5 inch squares from the napkin fabric.

Cut around the chosen details from the print feature. To make the napkins, fold over ¼ inch twice on all the napkin edges and topstitch all around close to the edges to hem.

Have the right side of the napkin up and place it flat and pin-ric-rac around all edges (1/2 inch from the edge. Use matching thread to stitch in place).

Use the fusible web to make 4 fussy cut circles and center the circles at about 1.5 inches from the bottom and in from the right. Use your machine (or hand) to blanket stitch. Repeat this to make four napkins in total.

3: Chapstick Holder Keychain Pattern

Supplies

- Chapstick

- A small scrap of fabric

- Keychain ring

Procedure

Begin by cutting your fabric- you will only need one piece. Cut the fabric at about 3.5 inches wide and 9 inches long.

Fold the fabric in half, right sides together, and sew along the sides.

Turn the fabric such that the right side is out and press flat with the seam on just one side.

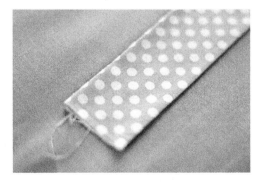

Stitch a hem on one edge by folding under by about half an inch, pressing flat, then folding under another half an inch. Press flat and stitch across that spot.

At this point, simply flip your holder over to work on the other side. Hem the other end and fold a few inches to leave just an inch or two left at the top.

Sew both sides of the section you folded up. Here is a back view:

Thread the top hem through your keyring, and voila: Easy-peasy!

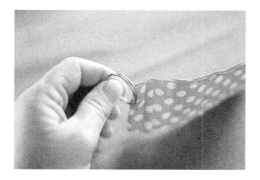

4: Beer Holder

Supplies

- (2) 11×5 inches pieces fusible fleece

- Point turning tool

- 11×5 inches piece quilting cotton (for the body lining)

- Denim sewing needle

- 11×5 inches piece Insulbright (this heavy-duty insulated fleece is found with the stabilizers and interfacings)

- 4.25 inches piece of 1.5 inches Velcro

- Coordinating thread

- Basic sewing supplies like machine, iron, pins, etc.

- 11×5 inches piece quilting cotton (for the outer body)

Procedure

Start by fusing a piece of fleece with the wrong sides of the outer lining body pieces as per the manufactures' recommendations.

Make sure the outer body piece is facing up on a surface and then proceed to lay the body lining piece with the face down on the piece. Make sure to align edges. Have the Insulbright piece on the top of the other layers, ensuring that the raw edges align perfectly. Pin this in place.

Fit the denim sewing needle in your sewing machine, and with a seam allowance of ¼ an inch, stitch around the stacked pieces of fabric, leaving only a 3 inch opening on one of the short ends.

Clip corners and cut the seam to 1/8 inches but leave the end with the opening untrimmed.

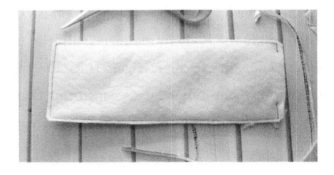

Use the opening you left to turn your work right-side out— use a corner turning tool to ensure the corners are sharp. Press your koozies perfectly and pin shut the opening.

Edgestitch all around your piece, shutting the opening as you sew.

Align the hook part of the Velcro around the left edge to the front side of the koozie and pin in place. Piece all around the four edges of the Velcro to secure, then align the loop part of the Velcro along the backside of the koozie. Pin in place and then stitch and stitch around the four edges to secure. And you are done!

5: Baby Bib

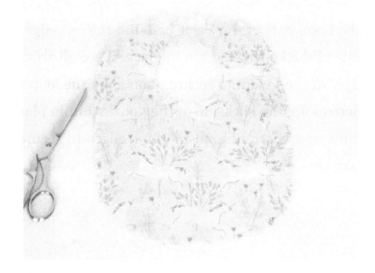

Supplies

- Snaps or Velcro

- Baby Bib Pattern

- Matching Thread

- Pins

- 2- 1/2 yard cuts of flannel fabric (yields 2 bibs)

Procedure

Print and tape together your baby bib pattern. Cut out individual pattern pieces and align the two pieces of small triangles together.

Pin the patterns to the fabric and cut around the pattern. A bib needs two pieces of fabric; remember that if you will be making many sets.

Think about using pieces of fabric that coordinate since the bib will be reversible. Lay the pieces of fabric with the wrong sides together and pin. You can always draw a line around the bib's edge to guide you while sewing—if sewing on rounded edges feels a bit challenging for you, remember to use the correct marking tools.

Begin at the bottom and sew up, then around the neck area up to the beginning where you started, then backstitch to secure.

To make the fringe cut close to the stitching (but not through!) every quarter an inch all around the bib.

Place a snap half an inch from the stitching line on both sides of the bib. You can also use a 1-inch piece of Velcro if you don't want snaps.

Put your bibs in the dryer to get your fluff on, and that's it!

Conclusion

Sewing is easy and exciting, and as long as you have this guide by your side, you will enjoy every step of it.

Just make sure to follow the guide step by step and start with easy stitches before you start working on bigger projects. Remember that practice makes perfect!

Good luck!

Made in the USA
Las Vegas, NV
11 January 2024

84226981R00089